ALL THE REAL

For Mum, who liked poetry

Also by Peter Bennet

First Impressions, with Rosemary Scott and Dave Stagg
(Mandeville Press)

Sky-Riding (Peterloo Poets)

The Border Hunt (Jackson's Arm)

A Clee Sequence (Lincolnshire and Humberside Arts)

ALL THE REAL

Peter Bennet

FLAMBARD

ACKNOWLEDGEMENTS

Some of these poems have appeared in the following magazines, pamphlets and books: *Bête Noire, Big Little Poems, The Border Hunt, A Clee Sequence, The Echo Room, High on the Walls, Key Words, Newcastle Evening Chronicle, Poetry Durham, The Poetry Book Society Anthology 2, Poetry Matters, The Rialto* and *Tide Lines*. 'Sir John Fenwick's Skull, Hexham Abbey' won the Basil Bunting Award in 1987.

The painting reproduced on the front cover is *November: Towards Shap* by Karen Wallbank. David Seymour's photograph of Bernard Berenson is reproduced by permission of Magnum Photos Ltd.

Flambard Press wishes to thank Northern Arts for its financial support.

Published in 1994 by Flambard Press
4 Mitchell Avenue, Jesmond, Newcastle upon Tyne NE2 3LA

Typeset by Pandon Press Ltd, Newcastle upon Tyne
in association with Mary Holcroft Veitch
Printed in Great Britain by Cromwell Press, Broughton Gifford,
Melksham, Wiltshire

A CIP catalogue record for this book is available from the British Library
ISBN 1 873226 07 1
© Peter Bennet 1994

CONTENTS

The may is out.
From underneath its skirt, new lambs
    have dashed from shadow into thought.

Thought travels fast.
The hawthorn is a stripped machine
    that turns its axle into rust.

ALL THE REAL

The road is heading straight for cloud –
this afternoon, I'm sceptical.

There is no fell beyond the rise, no cottage
for me to be at home alone,
no books, no pots and pans, no cat,
no Teacher's and no bottle either.

Yet two men balance on the skin
of Sweethope Lough,
and even when I steal their dinghy
to shoe four feet in one trim metaphor, they stay
companionably casting
trout flies at their twin reflections
on a surface like my mind.

And all the real fish are rising.

NOT AT HOME

for Richard Kell

You ask for poems built like walls
against the infiltrating frost, the purple
storms of rhetoric.

I'd choose windows, craftily reflecting
each Peeping Tom.

But strong walls crumple,
and glass melts into scorching tears,
as soon as I move closer and peer through
to that small room
Erato and Calliope share –
the broken stylus and the rickety lyre,
and all that mail on the mat.

THIS ROAD, THIS ARGUMENT

Someone went through again last night
along this road, this argument.

How urgently
the slack hand on the wheel, the heavy foot,
ask to seem as though they meant it.

This is a dangerous route, not just a necklace
of lonely farms –
more like a cord as tight across a parcel
of moorland and plantation
as meaning ties action. And always, here,
because a small burn spent such ages
licking rock, we tumble to a narrow bridge
and error, maybe –
skid marks and a little glass.

If death's the merest accident,
is life another? This road, this argument,
is after all predictable –
always the same trap, sudden, well-concealed,
that jerks the cord and lets the gut unravel.

HARESHAW LINN

is inching nearer
its beginning.

However hard its teeth are gritted,
stone is bitten. Water fumes,
squeezed by its entourage of oak, of beech –
earth lifter, rummaging in spate.

Among this crockery of cliffs,
outriding trees
have dangled wishbones of their dead
like timber lightning.
Resentful of your footsteps, they
discharge, through loopholes in the rock,
their weaponry
in bursts of rooks.

There's no way home
except the route you got here by.

Go back.

High moorland has been scoured for snow,
the melt
leans forward in an upright thunder.

Sandstone pressure
bends rainbows to the neck of water.

CLEARING THE SPRING

Two gale-thumped spruce have jammed the path
since I was here a year ago,
the rest are swordsmen,
jabbing for the face, the eye.

I'm D'Artagnan, my saw prevails –
spiked limbs are lopped and hauled away.

The spring itself is oily tea,
its surface breeding.

I shovel mud until the outflow
chuckles, catching light,
and then look down
at clearing water and my own sweat rising
darkly from an older me.

I'll lug it home across the fell,
and drink it, wash in it,
grow younger.

FROST AT COTE BOTTOM

At dusk, we climbed to check the hose
down from the spring. Each step was hoiked
from slither, snatching at bent grass
for purchase, bitter cold. Now snug

between two stoves, we speculate
about the kinship of the words:
heart, so nearly hearth – the softer
consonant repeated in the slide

of heat through wristy copper
and radiators bought as scrap
but pulsing life, so nearly love
that no hope carried here will drop

stillborn, but thrive, despite the frost
in Bishopdale, this cold placenta
that cheats the thin umbilicus
of water, so nearly winter.

BONFIRE AT COTE BOTTOM

The children spend an hour
collecting, soon
they've made a firefall cascade
upside down from cardboard boxes
ghosting into corduroy.

This is what kids are for,
says someone, meaning
that we can flicker into childhood too.
Or aboriginality,
that winkles us from private caves.
Not playful, rapt.
And smirking at this element
by which we're haloed to our heels,
and reaching
to match the stature of our shadows.

Smoke wags its tails and kisses faces
rosy with antiquity,
and safe from all the night is full of.

Later, I'm back,
the odd one of the tribe again,
to watch the embers shrivel, and frost ease
clouds into an opening
through which the last cold sparks escape
to start afresh as constellations.

LOOKING TOWARDS KIELDER

December hoards its light.
Shadows fumble
through all the moorland's empty pockets.

Perhaps I'll go, with one huge stride,
to where the sun
is spending like a drunken sailor.

One foot's a migratory goose,
the other hauls
its long wake on a tideless ocean.

Two magpies haggle on my wall –
they'll never quit
until they've sold each other something.

Perhaps I'll stay, eyes on the gloaming,
hands in pockets,
as if my shoes were tied together.

MAGPIES

Coveting the brightness, maybe,
of their reflections,
they're tapping Morse code on my window,
meaning luck
and sober morning
all the way to Carter Bar.

A two-bird crowd –
they jostle like a rowdy party
of Champagne Charlies
arriving at the wrong address.

Except their sliding eyes aren't bleary.

REDSHANK

for Norman MacCaig

The saltmarsh is a doormat
not to step on,
for all the sea is acting friendly.

Where someone daubed
ALL MEN ARE EQUAL IN THE EYES OF GOD
around the one
eye of a concrete pillbox,
a redshank squeaks its brand-new shoes
across the corner of God's ear.

TESTING TANKS ON CHESTERHOPE

Land-lice hauling ochre clouds
churn moorland into battle tracks.

This always was a cut-throat place –
Northumberland,
the old stiff neck of Britain.

It's all so vilely eloquent,
this war dance of technology,
this bump and grind
that has the skrike of sawmills in it,
the grunt of pigs.

It's not the metal or the ground that speaks.

HOPEFUL

The van slides to a tilt
on winter moorland,
and settles at a distance like a neat
blue package
on a crumpled khaki eiderdown.

I think of Santa Claus,
and me being less than half my size, but twice
as full of expectation.

It's Thompson,
with one wheel off the road again,
and Calor gas,
to keep the cottage feeling cosy.

I think of years, and icy journeys.

I want to take a sweater off,
and open each room like a present
with a bright new future in it,
not huddle in the only spot it's really warm,
the past.

WINTER HILLS

Beyond the lichened balustrade, I saw
my parents on a shelving lawn,
one Saturday, the start of summer.

Though men cut timber in the higher woods,
and children squawked from shrubberies,
a twang of insects dulled each sound.

He wore his khaki, she the soft print dress
that's famous in the photographs –
they glanced towards me joyfully, and smiled.

But I am not the one that they remembered,
and only I can see the birches bend
across the slope where they embraced each other,

and how the winter hills close round.

REVENANTS

Dust is in the picnic basket
they swing between them as they ramble
hills whose bellows-leather wings
bleach in a birdless estuary.

They're young again, so much in love,
they pass the castle built of lead,
with iron quoins that rust like blood,
not noticing its gates swing open.

Now they stroll across their garden,
towards the oak tree on the lawn for ever,
as darkness settles on the pond
of sticklebacks and water boatmen.

THE WISHING STONE

Embarrassing outside a
tidy cottage –
the wishing stone squats on the nubbles

of its stump. It might have been a tree,
this monarch,
flattered by a court of pebbles.

Lightbulb-sized sea-smoothies, those,
compared with which
the rock packs megawatts.

A fissure like an axe wound in the top
must be the place you have to spit...
Is someone looking?

Quickly, I lick a finger
and apply saliva in a leaf-shaped dab.
I'm moving

my left hand round three times, pretending
to be looking at my watch. My wish
is roots and branches.

DUDDO STONES

for my wife

Summer grips us in its damp
grey palm. But there, across a quarter-mile
of perfect wheat, are blinks of sunlight choosing,
one by one, grooved faces of five megaliths
to celebrate, beyond the wind-stroked crop
that balks us, and by balking speaks
for stones whose prime contemporary role
is surely the dumb oracle.

We'll hike back here at harvest time
to put more closely what it is
we can't quite ask,
and meanwhile leave, beside untrodden wheat,
a miserly libation
of lukewarm coffee from a Thermos flask.

HIGH SUMMER

Silence operates a timeless system
in which the grazed hills are content
to be unnamed, or call themselves Arcadia.

The mind's school is on holiday.

Just you and I, and one lost bumblebee,
to show the goddesses and gods around
the treacle-varnished corridors,
the gym, the playing fields,
and offer pollen, and our inky hands.

AFTER DARK IN THE PLAYING FIELDS

Play empties into lighted classrooms,
leaving dark
where winter birds have stayed awake

in air left hollow by the children's clatter. They
are quiet, hardly visible,
seen only by the bread they carry, strung

like tatters in a net of wind,
equally dark,
which hunger is unravelling.

FACE PAINTING AT THREPWOOD HILL

for Linda France

This child will not be the first
to dream his parents in a garden,
young and smiling, fond and close,
standing as they are before him.

Wind churns gouts of elder blossom,
tosses just the kind of salad
Eden was. Land curls its pages
like Genesis towards the Tyne,
that forked tongue snaking to the sea.

Half-afraid to be the beast
squiggles on his face have made him,
he threatens through a mask of smears
to eat the world, including them.

He will, and after comes the dream.

AN OBJECT IN THE BRITISH MUSEUM

John Dee's Aztec curio –
surely the closest that a stone can come
to vacancy –
sits propped up in its cabinet,
dulling like an empty sun.

It's not absurd of Dr Dee
to think he saw the Devil peeping
out from dark obsidian.

I see him too.

His face is like uncertainty
of all but slow paralysis
of body and of love, of reason also.

Put all against my looking glass,
the Devil whispers,
and it shows hollow.

That's how this emperor twists
the fairy tale –
his clothes exist without him, just
weft and warp across the mirror,
snagging the thinking fingernail.

FIVE AFTER GRIMM

1 *Sleeping Beauty*

The scullion,
who watched the cook's big fist
come slowly down
as if through water as he fell asleep,
has settled into cowering rage.

Blue flies are welded into trance
so fixedly, that we
press through them with our noses,
and through the walls they're jewelling, to prove
how easily a palace can dissolve.

Cats snooze.

Rats sprawl.

Peacocks doze on terraces,
tails ablaze,
and courtiers are effigies
of rank and enmity.

The king and queen
preside like waxworks, dustily indulging
our close, gigantic faces.

The princess, pricked asleep
beside her spindle,
smiles in complicity.

Her dreams unweave
the vile quickthorn, choked with suitors.

Her finger will be bleeding when she wakes.

2 *Red Riding Hood*

Feet slip in a mushroom-cobbled
gloaming, though morning lolls,
fakir-fashion,
across the high spikes of the pines.

The hank of smoke from Grandma's hearth
is tinsel,
snagged in a dell,
and snaking like the path we're following.

Our scarlet girl
dreams shaggy hair and smiling snarl
to gobble her deliciously,
and not the unfaked spikes of pain
Grandma hasn't told her of.

Take care.

The glow-worm light of our attention casts
wolfish shadows on the page.

3 *The Frog Prince*

A wet patch on your bedroom windowsill,
a hop towards you where you sleep, is me
whose body is a parody of yours,
just as your golden tennis balls were not
unlike the yellow bubbles of my breath
when I went diving for you into swills
your thoughts are careful to avoid. How quick
you were to bargain with a frog, as if
your toys were unrenewable and held
you spellbound in your chains of beauty
as I am spellbound into loathsomeness.
This eloquence alone is evidence
of princely status, lost, of course, unless
you gratify my sharp desire to stretch
snug on the pillow, warming at your breath
a frog-shape lithe and slippery enough
to enter you at last, like royalty.

4 *Rapunzel*

Your tower steals colour
as the hours pass,
was dental in moonlight, drab at dawn,
and blushes like lipstick now the sun
sinks down behind our book
of fairy tales.

Indeed, your lips could not seem
brighter, in this light,
or more resemble petals, which they are,
pursed now like a human kiss
against your side of the page,
our one-way mirror.

We relish this intimate surveillance.

It's dark now, but your roots are glistening
earthwards as the mirror dims.

The abseiling witch and gormless
clambering prince
begin to climb your tower of words.

You're not a good girl,
Miss *Campanula Rapunculus.*

Generations will have been your jailers
before you shrivel
and your unread lips
blow drily from your teeth like potpourri.

5 *Cinderella*

Your stepmother has made a mutt of him,
while I, already cold before I died,
lay under snow. The earth is warming now,
and soon the branch you pressed into the grave
as if it were my final crazy plume
will foliate and spread itself to house
the kind and spiritual birds. Its roots
would rap the coffin lid if I should fail
to talk in my imaginary sleep.
Meanwhile, he skirts the shadows of the hearth
avoiding you, undaughterly in rags
fastidiously bought at jumble sales.
Women who won't look glad when he's about
dilute his happiness. Oh dear,
how much your so-called sisters disapprove,
while polishing their nails and swapping shoes.
No wonder you do all the skivvying.
But, where you hide yourself among the dross,
transmutation starts. Despair's a furnace.
The kitchen, like an alembic, distils
your female potency to fairy tale.

IN FACT

The sun completes an idle winter lob,
as if thrown
for a puppy to bring back
in time for morning.

It does all this while being truthful.

Frost, that glitters from the hollows
it spent the whole day
lying in,
is also always very truthful.

The hills will change from Robin Hood green
to Snow White white,
without ever having been a fairy tale.

POOR JACK

Mist leaves a line of hilltops stranded
halfway up the sky, and looking
shiftily aesthetic.

It's Jack-in-the-Beanstalk-Land, except
the giant will be *distingué*
and vague,
a connoisseur of oriental art.

The rosebush wags a prickly English paw,
as though to say,
You'd better shin up
and fetch the poor lad down again
before he takes to wearing silk pyjamas,
and writing haiku.

ANOTHER MOMENT

I'm peering through a threadbare rainbow,
spider-tied
from washing line to dewy lawn,
to where a cat's paw lifts and stretches.

The little madame
pauses as her claws touch wood,
and looks at me as if to say,
There's another moment botched
because you saw it.

Here come two jumpers
and a drip-dry skirt.

I watch them weep.

DEAF CAT

When I touched him, dull responses,
and not much cat beneath those dreadlocks –
behind the petrol-coloured eyes,
his brain and ears are disconnected.

Like dirty cumulus, he's drifting
across the paths of hooting cars,
and pouncing, as a cloud should not,
to catch my breath between his paws.

FIRST CALF

for Maggie Bede

1

No pasture yet, a threshing floor
where wind beats chaff

from skittered snow. A half-light, spinning,
finds but will not warm at all

her blunt head,
levelled like a ram,

stretch-mouthed for an aria.
From bagpipe on her four black legs, the first

calf of the year is dropping,
swaddled into blood, but dying.

2

Stumble-foot, man snatches rope –
the dragged scrap makes for simple drawing,

zigzag on the fellside slope,
a fragile trace

which solemnly treads out to nothing.
Every step the mother, licking,

calls full-throated in the hush
of storm blown inside out. The sky

is veined like afterbirth, too wide and red
for such a meagre tragedy.

SWIMMING RABBIT

Conversation silvers as
the sea does, pinching Lindisfarne –
first ankle-deep, then getting risky.

A little struggle, rabbit-shaped,
swims from you to me. I think
its ears are waterlogged, but flattened
to float its nose along the water.

How does it know what strokes to use?
Or me? Or you?

Yet this scrap, with its fur bedraggled,
arrives triumphantly, displacing
all the oceans I imagine.

MOON FOX

A fox jumps off the wall and stabs
through snow across the rabbit ground.

His going is a sudden itch,
a tickle of the bandaged face
of moorland gawping at the moon.

He is the moon's familiar,
his brush the sickle's opposite.

THE BORDER HUNT

Release your fox
and let her run.

The thin, sharp grasses will extend
as if the ground anticipates
its landscape lover.

Rest your elbows on the warm
stone wall, the limit
of this foursquare earth I think
I am entitled to.

Or else lie down
where legal thickets keep us safe
to gaze out slantwise at the sprawl
of Cowstand Hill
and all that pother gathered on it.

Look, use binoculars
to make a trap door of your eyes –
quite soon
exciting things will tumble through.

I like this summoning
hoof murmur entering the blood.

You are so near.

Your sky (my bracken) cracks
with light.

Rough pasture strains and quivers like
your fox now running live
among her unguessed whereabouts.

It's better to conceive of this
as love, if only
for the poem's sake, and then
admit to blunt need suddenly
as flocks disperse like cream on tweed
to make room for the headlong throats
of Border hounds
belling on their threads of scent.

My Border Hunt
are landscape lovers sweating hard,
their buff and blue
a tide race on the sea of bents.

Indulge this loving
that would love to kill.

The hounds will soon be called away
to kennel straw through toy-town brass,
the hunt reduced
to hoof taps on a darkened road.

Death lines snap.

While fells adjust
their crumpled purple skirts,
the sun gets down to teasing out
shadows from a reiving clan.

Knees touch while tired horses breathe.

Elsewhere, along the Curtis Burn,
a fox is stepping
up from water onto stone.

NORTHERN PLACES

1 *Durham*

So scrutable a bulk of stone
tends shadow like a chiselled dial
whose gnomon, anchored to the heart
of pit heap, river, street and field,
keeps time embattled on the town.

2 *Langley Park*

This poor pit widow tucks a shawl
of coal smoke round her cottages.
Underneath, the poet's small
pick knocks for images –
top-quality, combustible.

3 *Consett*

Though spoil heaps will be planted, all
these streets extend to absences.
To slay the giant on the hill,
sandblast the blood dust off his face
and try to make him beautiful.

4 *Newcastle upon Tyne*

Longbows are bent against the sky –
a road sprung to a metal hull
projects their freight through snarls of chimneys.
Below, the river's unschooled pull
deflects the city's archery.

5 *Tynemouth*

Rampart, ditch and priory –
unlike their paying visitor –
are not bamboozled when the sea
revamps, behind the broken choir,
the plainsong of artillery.

DRURIDGE

Druridge Bay, on the Northumberland coast,
is a proposed site for a nuclear power station.

The bay's a lonely, windswept lung –
no arc lights leering, no barbed fences,
nothing poisoned yet awhile.

Evening still has leeway here
to let things slip their shapes and folk
be inward and a little humble.

This won't stop us.

That humped glare isn't sunrise,
it's the city.

Until we learn to do with less,
and trust the dark,
we're in on the conspiracy.

Our oceans smack their lips and sicken.

AT WALLINGTON HALL

Park trees cropped to parallel the ground
are dreaming cumulus, whose lower sides
the wind planes, without joy or anger.

I am a reasonable man.

Meanwhile, above these orderly umbrellas,
the whole stiltwalking world of vapour rests
on something nervous of the light,
that hurls each flouncing sycamore
towards me on a dark ellipse.

AIRSHIPS AND UMBRELLAS AT CRAMLINGTON

1

In Tibet, a floating boulder,
big as an airship,
tame as an umbrella,
shadows the eggshell heads of monks,
whose prayers, the rumour goes,
won't let it sink.

For, if it does,
the world sinks with it,
and no map reveals its whereabouts.

So don't trust maps.

They leave unclear
what little truth we fold inside them.

The Town Guide shows a mortgaged maze.

No sign of knee-thick, here-since-Domesday hedges
still busy splicing earth to air
in corners where the streets unzip.

2

What's past, the mind's eye makes a present of.

Biplanes, for instance, clamber air,
and coal-black marras howk and blast
underneath a level crust
of whitewashed hangars, pitheads, brickworks.

A brand-new Zeppelin bombs the fields,
and later, in the General Strike,
nine colliers will overturn
the Flying Scotsman, crewed by blacklegs.

It's nearly gone.

Coalspeak survives, coal villages
are raisins in an urban pudding.

But future here was mapped out cold
by someone at a drawing board,
who left no peg
to hang the soul's umbrella on.

AT ALNWICK CASTLE

The gates are closing for the day,
stoppering the way through battlemented stone
to ducal privacy.

Outside, I think of being humble.

My own ramparts have a tendency to tumble
in heavy rain, or lose
their top stones to an itchy cow.

But walls constrain us anyway.

What's best is looking out-over or in-over,
surviving as these trees do here,
like discharged prisoners,
uneasy in their suits of freshening green.

AT THE QUEEN'S HALL, HEXHAM

for John Harle

As silent as a catafalque,
the grand piano points its toes,
demurely underpinning bulk.

A mourner (sorry) pianist
and pageboy, tallow-blond and mute,
likewise extend their toes and wrists

towards their hope, the hierophant,
assured (if even art decays)
that one soprano saxophone

will blow the furnace doors, and blaze.

SIR JOHN FENWICK'S SKULL, HEXHAM ABBEY

Here's a voice,
though no sound is attached to it.

For years, a blown egg in a hatbox,
while choirboys picked away its teeth
and poked the fracture
that let the yolk and white escape
of who it thought it might have been
or what it died for.

It's speaking
out of a glass case now,
a purple cloth
tucked round it like a collier's muffler.

Time is getting fainter here –
shouts in the marketplace outside began
longer ago than Marston Moor.

Imagine it brags about the battle: *I spurred*
my horse to aid Prince Rupert and
struck and struck and struck again…
the sky fell and the ground came up…

But skulls don't tell you things like that –
they only say, *Remember Death.*

Or most skulls do.

This one prefers to be an egg
whose mother is a helmet-hen
that split in giving birth, still roosting
high on the south wall of the nave.

I think it says, *Remember Life.*

ARSON AT TYNEMOUTH PRIORY

There's old Cutquill, tonsured skull.
His tattered parchment-scrap of wall
is blotted by erosion, thumbed
to brain-stone by enquiring air.

Here's young Gluesnout, empty head.
This Viking leaves the brow of water
calm, unfurrowed by his coming.
His flame is simple, like a prayer.

THE OLD MOOR HOUSE

To navigate, the top clump of a scoured copse,
acoustic, when the wind allows
for twitterings –
just now, incorrigible hush.

The haunted inn is farther still,
good stone not quite tottering,
a roofless reticence preserved
in nettle smell.

They couldn't stop the murders here, despite
a gibbet opposite the door.

But there's no fright for me from what persists.

That hoof fall and that snort of breath
are just a thin girl on a white-faced pony,
leading another, riderless.

GALLOWGATE

At the electrician's, granite chunks
elbow from the showroom wall
among the light bulbs and alarm clocks.

Here, by the bus stop,
is where they used to bring miscreants,
desperate or just plain daft,
to hang outside the city limits
among the ash heaps and the middens.

Like dentists, hangmen
can be kind and quick, unless
you end up with a trainee or a bodger.

I just want a drive belt for the Hoover,
a small black noose.

But time keeps asking me to notice
how it flies,
and how it swings, kicking its legs.

SAD COMPANION

Behind the wood that I know best, the sun
is warming Aid Crag on its friendly side.
I think I hear that doves are cooing.

But I'm not there. I'm here, alongside
him from the outskirts, asking me
Where is the General Hospital, and how to cross
this city on his own tired feet.

It's in his look that it's a death he's due
to meet there in his shabby best.

I offer him the bus fare. He says *No*.

He'll climb up Westgate Hill from our encounter,
and carry off a bit of me, because
he chose me from the crowd to ask
which way he should be going with his worry.

I'll take him with me too, next time I pass
to heather slopes
through packed-out Norway spruce, to hear
the long sigh of the wind embraced by trees.

CUDDY'S WELL

St Cuthbert left the healing virtue
we joked about, and didn't look for.
No one saw your illness coming
that day when Hodgson's men were at the pant
mucking out a squat farm trailer.

Their stirrup pumps and buckets stoked a blaze
of rainbows, and their calls of laughter
might have been an intercession.
They stood like priests to let us drink, their hoses
spiring arcs of holy water.

CANCER PATIENT

Prune them hard, she says,
her treatment over,
advising me on raspberries.

I think instead
back to my opposite of gardens –
railway cuttings
scorched the height of their steep sides
and sometimes wild raspberries,
smouldering in their coils like fuses,
contriving green.

THE INVALID

Waking, as always, in her chair,
she watched the young man climb the street.
Light flamed the edges of his hair
as though it were the source of light.

He kept a little piece of card
cupped into his open hand,
scrutinising each facade
then glancing at his palm again.

He beamed and shone as though he held
a golden secret scribbled there.
She found a smile and almost felt
she knew who he was looking for.

But afterwards she dreamed the moon
came tracking down her own address.
It gripped the scrap her name was on
and pressed its face against the glass.

MID-LIFE CRISIS BY THE REDE

The pub was warm. She'd slipped outside –
a Pearly Queen
by courtesy of easy rain.

She walked a bit and recognised
a stone cut roughly for a lintel, proud
among the common river boulders,
its broken promise
cloaked in mossy uniform.

No one noticed she'd exchanged
our babble for the slow reproach
of stone and water.

WINSTON

His earth-caked feet are slightly odd –
one breaks bones, is accurate,
the other drags in slow half-moons.

Motionless, they're in cahoots
to badger at the battered head
he cocks at far-off, hopeless trains
with shivers from the loam he hates.

Society has banged the lid on.

Now he'll murder with his hoe
each cabbage in the prison garden.

NEIGHBOUR

It's midnight, but he keeps on knocking,
thumping like a failing heart –

TAPATAP, BUMPBUMP (and then the big one) BAM.

A hammer clatters to the deck.
He's jacked it in, thank God. And yet
how suddenly it's still and dark.
Work echoes every other work,
and, when it stops, the echoes slam
like all work stopping –

TAPATAP, BUMPBUMP (and then the big one) BAM.

BEANPOLE AND SHORTY

Beanpole seems to dip and rise
while Shorty sleepwalks, both are blobbed
like figures partly realised
against the background of a daub

crammed full of allegoric gloom.
They are themselves, but represent
the viewer also, in his room
outside the canvas. We enter

foreground to be there. It's late. The bus concourse
is empty, nearly – a crust
of tarmac, litter that could symbolise
the dump of present into past

with Friday nights when I had hair
but, callow, walked out dressed in stuff
like these museum pieces wear.
Drape jacket, bootlace, velvet cuffs –

a strange bird-legged silhouette,
thin Lynn Chadwick artefact
astride the Fifties,
shouldering the century into its second act.

Beanpole has a limp with which
his Tony Curtis, like the crest
of some sad warrior, flaps oddly. He touches
Shorty's tattooed wrist

to guide him, poor blind man,
towards this space the painter made.
Poor blind, poor skeleton,
they threaten nothing, yet I feel afraid.

BURGER BAR

The menu
has jolly pictures on its wipe-clean pages,
and playschool print.

Across the city, streetlights hiccup
into life,
and fog and night descend together
like funeral guests.

Passers-by peer sulphurously in
at where I'm sitting,
happily infantilised
by waitresses like bossy twelve-year-olds.

Music cracks and pops. A bank of screens
flaps simultaneous pelvic thrusts.

It's Shangri-la, and better
to be eating here
than join the scarecrow crowd outside.

They want my blood.

Poor ancestors,
who dine in cold and silent places.

A LIQUORICE CROWBAR

jars me a cobblestone
from other darkness, sweet black tar
slopping from its long-nosed can
a smoke cure for catarrh.

It's from a pavement firm enough
to walk the mind on,
blacked up round the mouth like Jolson
in reverse. Look closer,
soften childhood in the palm,
X-textured from the cooling tray to snakeskin –
small Black Mamba,
not biting till the past has levered
squeakily against my gum.

EXTRACTION

Houses, like teeth,
seem bigger than the space they occupy.

They hold so much
love, for instance, and its slow goodbye,
then leave no Where at all,
a blank
for dock and rosebay willowherb.

And both can still be visited.

I tongue the dimple in my gum –
a little well
that offers me my blood for tasting,
out of pity for myself.

LOGAN STREET

for Anne Stevenson

The hearth's a chatterbox. Wind slouches,
eavesdropping, borrowing a voice.
Floorboards concur. The walls are itching
beneath their plaster to converse.

You offered all there is of welcome
to this house at the point of speech. I'm mooching
at home among your rooms, your books. My thumb
is loosening the tongues of latches.

PRIME MERIDIAN

This silt is lisping,
Alone again and who would want you?

Lips among a wrack of flotsam
confide identity
as one half of a set of headphones
tasting of salt.

But what a rich world can be charted
from this beginning –
0° at Humberston
shall be my reference for new meridians
converging at the fertile poles
which need no one but me to map them.

FOR A GODSON

for David Thirsk

Easter Sunday
is filling up with spring and sermons.

I'm ironing my trousers, David,
to stand behind you at your christening.

In the corner of your Gran's kitchen window,
Stockport is tickled by sun. A plane
is flying in between
the window frame and all the toothy chimneys
of Crosby Street.

The plane is yours.
There is a bigger slice of blue
for you to fly
happily and wisely in.

Today is long ago
now that you are old enough to read.
Sun still shines
on Osborne Road and Crosby Street,
and the plane I gave you
still travels when you think of it.

Like you, it's going far
and fast enough
to keep from falling.

FÜR VIVIEN

It's thanks to you,
and Ferguson's Keyboard Anthology *–*
those green notes from your green piano.

Seagulls hopping from a sewage pipe
are grey notes from a flute
each time
the tide slops nearer Berwick.

Silence is the shape they're playing.

In Bath, each time the organ tuner
calls the nickname
of a note,
resonance stamps out the echoes
strewn in the Abbey
by the last, huge resonance.

Fan vaults falter in the old fandango
they're dancing up there in the dust
with light from the clerestory.

Sounds like these don't need a shape.

I'm learning, in my travelling,
that incompleteness is just beauty
being friendly,
and trying to start a conversation.

THE TRUEST CELTS

for John Bennet, c.1700-1778, yeoman,
and all his forbears and descendants

The TV frames some rock piles
and some sheep,
and now a witch in dungarees
leans across her bicycle.

They're dressing wells in Derbyshire.

Wind, a brass band, and the vicar's prayers
are tugging at her explanation
about the truest Celts of all remaining
stealthily and undefeated
in caverns under Eldon Hill
and up among the stones on Kinder.

I like her myth.

Celts of the Dark Peak and the White
unite –
but claim no language and no nation,
no Troubles, and no heritage
beyond the guardianship of streams
this stained-glass window faked in petals
affirms above the coiling water.

THE MURROUGH LADY

1

Please do not ask him
to describe her body, he
did not look back again, perhaps
afraid to try.

That is his tragedy,
for very few have seen
her step free from her ground and weather,
her apple-green.

The world she wore
is strewn about him, nonetheless,
as he approximates her shape
with fetishes.

2

So tall the sleet clouds
rode with her, and wind
brought something of her voice within it, we
were scavenging her property –
at her arrival,
cringed like yard dogs, felt
her brisk blows quench our quarrelling,
and better so.

Such bones we squabbled for
were muddied up past nourishing –
such shrill disputes
were each one's own cries echoing.

She spoke to us
as silence does, to underlife
which could recall the simple speech,
and make some glottal recess twitch
to murmur, *Mistress, welcome home.*

Driving off the eager,
chose the strong,
awarding manhood in her way.

Widow of so many friends,
she overleans my arm,
resorts to rain as though to tears
for idle ground,
the tilth of which she must maintain.

If I accept her subtle life,
my bargain will be not to ask
the world prismatic,
knowledge striding like the light,
or money-love or woman-love,
but tenancy of rising fields.

And when the season tilts
on end, no share
of harvest,
but freedom of her inner rooms,
the muckyards and the granaries
of her imaginary farms.

Time taps my heart impatiently,
but she is girlish, without age,
far richer than we had supposed,
haughty always, cruel at the harnessing.

The bargain was agreed, perhaps.
I can remember
only the stink of breaking earth, the sting,
the ribbed yoke of her heavy plough.

Each night a half-sleep,
never waking
to reap the brightness and the singing.

3

We harnessed darkness
to our need.
Of all unpleasant duties there,
I most disliked
to pour the rivulets of gory bait
and listen
for slobbering among the traps.

Such hard work, killing. Even so,
her grave stayed empty but for seepage. Those
detailed to bury her returned
with rigmaroles
of windings left on hurdles, or
her body woken in miasma.
Our great fires singularly failed.

I shivered through the ritual.
Sometimes we heard
echoes of her hungry singing
entangling our manly shout.
But fear is not appropriate. Her build
is smaller, largely, than our own.
Often she seemed beautiful.

SKATE ISLAND

for Henry Roberts

The sea's been tickling their ribs all night
and they're still chuckling,
each tugging on a waterlogged balloon.

And now she's nudged them with her tide
to face the harbour mouth. The Sound of Bute
beckons like a kitchen door.

But still the boats will not go out,
although she promises her skirts to cling to,
and something sharp to cut their teeth on –

Skate Island on a pewter tray.

TARBERT

Hang the picture where you'll see it when you wake –
pinewoods, and the hills of real Argyll,
decent hearths uncorking smoke
above the harbour with its night-lights winking –
and then pretend it's not as lovely
as some drab street, or vandalised estate.

That would be crazy.

Just like the woman stepping from her green back door
into the pink dawn flooding from the water,
who wishes she was anywhere but here.

A PAINTING BY TURNER

The New Moon; or 'I've lost my boat, you shan't have your hoop'
(Tate Gallery, London)

White pup, black pup,
full of beans out from the pigment,
between a cloud tongue and a fang of cliff,
are lonely.

It's very lonely in this picture –
oddly,
since no one's short of company.

Two kids past their bedtime and that woman
wearing the stormy hat, for instance,
will squabble while the canvas lasts,
not noticing
the big sea reach to take them under.

Look, a palid brush stroke turns
into a moon that's blinkable
back to paint, then moon again.

The loiterer who thinks that he's alone,
down at the very edge of beach,
will find the shadow that he shouldn't have,
in this light, painted
to stand up all too close beside him.

Gustave Doré (woodblock cut by H. Pisan): one of 370 illustrations for
Louis Viardot's French translation of Cervantes, *L'ingénieux hidalgo
Don Quichotte de la Manche* (Paris, 1863)

AFTER DORÉ, AFTER CERVANTES

It's no use talking to the Don –
his tomes mislay the force of things
beneath the fuss of chivalry.
Meanwhile, this brewing storm will sink
the path, this pitching waste
extends as Doré meant it to.

Your head is still a farmyard, Sancho.
With hopes of new adventure, he
will flatter his ambition, you –
whose slow thoughts turn as pigs' snouts do
through cakes of dung – remember wringing
chickens' necks, the warm lap of a filling churn.

Wants grow less elaborate
as his grow more so: hero's rations, first
of all, then some accommodating girl –
or more than one –
your paunch well wedged, your bum exposed
to firelight in a country inn.

A snatch of truth
has been engraved, not that
told by Cervantes, but
that this is how such journeys are. Your boss
depends on you entirely, as
the gut feeds the careering brow –

And you complain, fat Sancho, yet
the two of you must make one man
with shadowy Cardenio,
whose hopscotch beckons up and on
to height which pressure of the burin only
lifts from turbulence of cloud.

Bernard Berenson at the Borghese Gallery, Rome, 1955
Photo: David Seymour

BERENSON AT THE BORGHESE

for Dominic

His beard is frosted eagerness,
whiter than the panama
so neatly garnished with a ribbon
black as his suit
among the shadows thrown by art.

Informed by light, and yet his eyes
seem bruised by seeing.

The odalisque
is languor and solidity –
her chevelure like coral at the nape,
her long back sinking,
rising almost,
across a marble ottoman.

His gaze is labour –
she is shiftless, splendidly
uninterested in her beauty.

Her age extends
beyond the age of stone or making.

At ninety, Berenson distils
the taste of Europe in his looking.

THE EXHIBITION OF THE ESQUIMAUX

In a sea of dark clothes, walrus faces
close in towards the makeshift gravel beach
where Uckaluk has stocked her mother's grave
with ingenuities in bone and stitched
hide which are her only history. She kneels
        as though to die among her dogs
        in plain view of a British whaler.

Ice and piety are inching nearer.
She is fifteen this winter and so scrawny
her limbs are thin as baleen. Captain Parker
will not weigh anchor with a single woman
so Memiadluk is chosen and the couple
are educated, cleansed and married,
        aboard the *Truelove* out of Hull.

When shown in Northern towns, the honeymooners
capture all hearts with their docility
and gratitude. *They are Raw Meat Eaters,*
Surgeon Gedney's handbill states, *Their Form is not*
dissimilar to that of the Quadroon,
        but note that, like the Hottentot,
        they have a Mild and Sad Expression.

These beneficiaries of British Rule subsist
only by Charity of Whaling Vessels.
Yet even they, supplied with Shot and Muskets,
might feed themselves and, furthermore, establish
by Trade in Hides and Oils of Seal and Whale
        such Commerce as would march abreast
        with Propagation of the Gospel.

Captain my father now, Surgeon my mother…
Twelve thousand walruses each paid one shilling
to hear her utter, and to see her consort
pose in his kayak with a spear. Real weather
whitens the arctic backdrop and time fades
        their image like an oleograph
        above the mantelpiece of trade.

LE PLAN DES PENNES

for Margaret and François

1

Up at the ancient settlement
it's hot white limestone gripping tinder,
Roman cart ruts and cigalles.

A mountain toothache lowers
a Boeing 737 towards
the wrecked cars and the quarries
round L'Estaque, against the light.

The airport is a tyre-smirched springboard
out into L'Étang de Berre,
it bounces grace,
stills a pirouette to jetsam.

Futures in a fan of cards
are peddled at the café tables.

The gendarme knows the gypsy's past,
her future also.

2

Pas là, not there –
though M. Pala isn't here,
his stud boar is.

Its pen is small, its penis big.

Bulk and stink are factual, its eyes
are roving, sailor-blue.

Tomorrow it escapes. Me too.

A little glare shaped like a trotter
waits on the pavement for my foot
to step on, into gold, below
the window of the restaurant
high in the Basilica de S. Victor
where a waiter offers to his sea, his city,
all the songs he has for nothing.

M. Pala flogs his pig
back from the village to its snout-deep wallow.

Pas là, not there –
he flogs himself
from cash to shit and back again,
no wiser.

3

Pleases and thankyous fill the crypt
like candles, like a shoal of crutches,
like model aeroplanes, like boats, like flowers
choked in cellophane.

Pas là, not there –
Christ's body is a waxy sprawl
islanded in candlelight,
a paper rose
pressed into the deepest wound.

4

Someone's kids are loud and early.

The gypsy moves her futures on,
her black skirt huge as in the dream
of flying.

Folding our after-party bed,
the pig and I
shake an image from the blanket –
two pyramids, a nude girl
of an antique kind –
La Terre, the card of the evangelists.

She has another guy in mind, and yet
it's possible to be in love –
n'est-ce pas? –
with cheap gilt sandles sloughed
while dancing,
the dust on them, a few dry leaves.

Together, all the dead contrive
to sing as one voice easily,
a deep, remembered, intonation.

And what they sing is most exact,
most truthful, since it has no words.
And what they sing is wise and kind.

Its kindness is the end of pain.
Its wisdom is that each birth frees
an accent from the song again.